LIVING WITH
CELIAC DISEASE

ABDO
Publishing Company

LIVING WITH CELIAC DISEASE

by Dale-Marie Bryan
Content Consultant
Devon Golem, Registered Dietitian,
Rutgers University, New Brunswick, New Jersey

LIVING WITH HEALTH CHALLENGES

CREDITS

Published by ABDO Publishing Company, PO Box 398166, Minneapolis, MN 55439. Copyright © 2012 by Abdo Consulting Group, Inc. International copyrights reserved in all countries. No part of this book may be reproduced in any form without written permission from the publisher. The Essential Library™ is a trademark and logo of ABDO Publishing Company.

Printed in the United States of America,
North Mankato, Minnesota
102011
012012

Editor: Holly Saari
Copy Editor: Karen Latchana Kenney
Series design and cover production: Becky Daum
Interior production: Kazuko Collins

Library of Congress Cataloging-in-Publication Data
Bryan, Dale-Marie, 1953-
  Living with celiac disease / by Dale-Marie Bryan.
     p. cm. -- (Living with health challenges)
  Includes bibliographical references.
  ISBN 978-1-61783-125-6
  1. Celiac disease--Juvenile literature. I. Title.
  RC862.C44B79 2012
  616.3'99--dc23
                                          2011033148

TABLE OF CONTENTS

EXPERT ADVICE

I have been a registered dietitian since 2003 and have worked in many clinical and counseling settings. I have counseled numerous individuals diagnosed with celiac disease. Teenagers are my most intriguing clients, as they tend to be in a dietetic transition period: they are making more food choices for themselves. Yet, as they are making more food choices, they have the additional challenge of managing a gluten-free diet.

It's important to remember that most individuals with celiac disease live healthy lives. You are not alone—there are many sources of information available, whether they are found in your community or on the Internet. My few key pieces of advice for you are:

Know what you consume. Read ingredient labels and communicate with appropriate professionals (cooks, chefs, food companies, pharmacists) to understand the gluten-content of food products, medications, and cosmetics that you consume and use.

Bring your own. Always carry a gluten-free snack with you so you always have something to eat. When eating in different settings, bring gluten-free food with you. Keep in mind that other individuals who are providing food may not be as knowledgeable when it comes to a gluten-free diet.

Enrich your gluten-free diet. Turn your focus to what you can eat. Include lots of fruits and vegetables, gluten-free whole grains, and lean proteins in your diet. Try new gluten-free foods and recipes. A little bit of research goes a long way to cultivating a varied, interesting, and healthy gluten-free diet.

There is good news for people with celiac disease: growing awareness of celiac disease by health-care professionals, the food industry, and researchers. The recognition of a new target market has promoted the food industry to create a variety of delicious, gluten-free products that are more widely available. Most important, growing awareness of this disease has promoted communication between diagnosed individuals. Being in contact with others like you makes it easier to live with celiac disease. You are not alone!

Like all lifestyle behavioral changes, the changes that accompany a diagnosis of celiac disease can appear tedious, overwhelming, and unfair. However, with consistency and time, these changes get easier. As your knowledge and experience expand, you begin to make healthy choices for yourself with ease.

—*Devon Golem, Registered Dietitian, Rutgers University, New Brunswick, New Jersey*

WHAT IS HAPPENING TO ME? DEFINING CELIAC DISEASE

"**A**ngie A. ♥ Alex G." For the third time since lunch, 15-year-old Brittany stared at the sappy message scratched on the bathroom stall door. Then she squeezed her eyes tightly as another spasm of pain and diarrhea overwhelmed her.

Moments later, the outer door banged open and girls' voices echoed in the bathroom. "Good grief!" one voice rose above the others. Brittany recognized it as Angie's. "It smells like someone died in here!"

Feels like it too, Brittany thought as tears of pain and embarrassment welled in her eyes. She wished she could lift her shoes so no one would recognize her in the farthest stall, but that would hurt her bloated belly too much.

All Brittany wanted was to go home and curl up in bed. She hated to call her mother again, and she'd already missed a lot of school throughout the year. Some days she was so tired she couldn't even get her body out of bed. But the way she felt, there was no way she could concentrate in class.

Maybe it was "in her head" as one doctor suggested. But how could that be? She wasn't imagining the sores in her mouth, the weight loss, or her aching joints. Sick as she often felt now, she was constantly hungry. She hardly recognized the pale face staring back at her in the mirror. Then there was the fatigue that left her limp as the spaghetti she'd eaten at lunch.

With so many things wrong, it was no wonder she was irritable and depressed. It didn't help that kids accused her of being bulimic—even her parents had wondered. But, thankfully, they and the latest doctor they'd consulted believed her. Now they were just waiting for the test results. She was bracing herself for the worst, but it would be a relief to finally know the name of the enemy that was attacking her.

CELIAC DISEASE DEFINED

After her test results came back, Brittany learned she had celiac disease, but she had no idea what it was, nor had she even heard of it before. Celiac disease, also called celiac sprue, is an autoimmune disorder, which means the immune system attacks the body's tissues instead of attacking foreign substances. The trigger for the attack is gluten, a protein found in wheat, barley, and rye, which are ingredients in many popular foods including pizza, bread, and the spaghetti Brittany ate for lunch.

MORE ABOUT GLUTEN

Gluten is the sticky stuff that forms when yeast combines with flour. It is the substance that gives bread its chewy texture and allows it to hold its shape. Even things such as soups, syrups, and flavorings can contain gluten. It is used in different food products for flavor or texture enhancement.

If you have celiac disease, the gluten in the bread on your sandwich causes your immune system to react abnormally.

WHO GETS CELIAC DISEASE?

You've never heard of celiac disease? You're not alone. Though it is estimated 1 percent of the US population, or one in 133 Americans, has the disease, 97 percent who have it have not been diagnosed. That means approximately 2.5 to 3 million people who shouldn't be eating foods such as pizza and bread are still eating them—and getting sick because of their diet.[1]

Celiac disease can develop at any age, and most often it occurs in a person with a particular genetic makeup. Some children exhibit symptoms right after they begin eating gluten, while others do not develop the disease until adulthood.

The most common denominator among people with celiac disease is having a particular gene. Genes are the determiners in cells that tell such things as your hair and eye color and whether you'll be stocky or slim. In the case of celiac disease, people with one of two particular genes called HLA DQ2 or DQ8 have a chance of developing celiac disease. Thirty to 40 percent of the North American population has these contributing genes, but only 2 to 3 percent of that number develops celiac disease. Only around 5 percent of people who do not have these genes develop the disease.[2]

SYMPTOMS

Celiac disease has many symptoms and several of them mimic other ailments. This is why diagnosing the disease is often so difficult. Symptoms in children can include pale skin, grumpiness, a bloated belly, smelly bowel movements, and stunted growth. Children may also fail to grow, have bone abnormalities, or develop a disease called rickets in which bone is not made, becomes soft, or is distorted. This is due to the child not being able to absorb calcium and vitamin D, both essential for bone building. Rickets may cause muscle weakness and bone pain. Children may also have weak enamel on their teeth, a delay in starting puberty, behavioral problems including restlessness and inattentiveness, or an itchy skin rash.

Young adults and adults may have complaints of diarrhea, bloating, and belly pain. But they may also experience constipation, excessive gas, and vomiting. Weight loss has long been thought of as a common symptom, but people with celiac disease can be overweight as well.

Depression and migraine headaches can also result from untreated celiac disease. If you are clinically depressed, you are experiencing intensely sad feelings. It is more than just feeling down or "blue." The feelings last longer than a few days and interfere with your daily

MYTHS ABOUT CELIAC DISEASE

1. *People can have borderline celiac disease.*
   No, you either have it or you don't.
2. *If you use shampoo that contains gluten, you'll get sick.*
   Not unless you drink it. The only gluten that will make you sick is gluten that is consumed.
3. *If you feel good, you don't have celiac disease.*
   Not true. You can have celiac disease with no symptoms.
4. *You can outgrow celiac disease.*
   Unfortunately, no. Your symptoms may subside after a time, but you still have it and need to eliminate gluten from your diet.

Frequent migraines could be an indication of celiac disease.

life. You may want to sleep all the time, and you may lose interest in activities you usually enjoy. One hypothesis for why some people with celiac disease have depression is that their damaged small intestines cannot properly absorb nutrients such as B_{12} and folate. Scientists know that low levels of these nutrients can negatively affect a person's mood, but they are still not certain if the low levels of these nutrients are what cause depression in people with celiac disease.

A migraine is a severe, throbbing headache that gets worse with movement, light, and sound and can be a symptom of celiac disease. Migraines keep you from doing your daily activities and can cause nausea and vision abnormalities. A 2003 study indicated that migraine sufferers have higher incidences of celiac disease.[3] People who have celiac disease and migraines often find they have fewer or less severe headaches once they stop eating gluten.

NOT AN ALLERGY

When you tell some people you have celiac disease, they might think you're allergic to gluten, but this is not the case. Celiac disease is not an allergy at all; however, both an allergy to gluten and celiac disease involve the immune system, which is why they are sometimes confused.

If you have celiac disease, your immune system attacks tissues in your body whenever you eat gluten. Celiac disease damages the small intestine over a long period of time and may not show up immediately. If you have an allergy to gluten, the reaction is immediate. Seconds or minutes after eating gluten, your immune system releases histamine into your bloodstream. You might become short of breath or your throat might swell. You might break out in hives or experience nausea, vomiting, or diarrhea. The easiest way to remember the difference between the two is that a food allergy shows symptoms quickly, while complications of celiac disease can take months or years to develop.

CELIAC DISEASE IS CHANGING AND INCREASING

Though there is still a lot scientists don't know about celiac disease, they are learning more about why people develop it. One thing they are finding is that the way celiac disease presents itself is changing. For example, in the past, children were more likely to get celiac disease. But now, adults are diagnosed more often.

The number of people getting the disease is increasing too. It is true that more people are being diagnosed, but that may be because testing is easier and more precise. Also, doctors have learned more about the disease, such as the gene-related factor and that the disease produces specific antibodies in the blood, making it easier to diagnose. But that doesn't explain the fact that more people are getting the disease today than in the past.

Once you have celiac disease, staying away from bread and other foods containing gluten will become a normal part of your life.

Scientists believe environmental factors play a part in the disease's development. But they haven't yet determined exactly what those factors are. A theory proposed in 1989 by British doctor David Strachan suggested that as a result of becoming so clean, we have fewer infections. This prevents our immune system from "practicing" its protection of our body. The immune system doesn't develop well enough to tell what to attack, so it instead attacks the body.

Dr. Joseph Murray at the Mayo Clinic thinks celiac disease could be related to the way wheat is currently processed and eaten. Processed foods we eat today were not available 50 years ago. Wheat has changed too. Early wheat strains didn't contain gliadin, which scientists know triggers the immune system to attack the small intestine.

LIVING WITH CELIAC DISEASE

There is much to learn about celiac disease and new discoveries are being made all the time. The key to coping is to learn all you can about the disease. Finding out you have celiac disease will change your life, but following a treatment plan and keeping up with new developments will help you make it a great life.

CELIAC DISEASE VERSUS FOOD ALLERGIES AND INTOLERANCES

Having celiac disease is not the same as being allergic or intolerant to a food. Celiac disease is an autoimmune disease, so the body attacks its own tissues. Food allergies elicit an immune system response, but the body attacks a usually harmless substance that is consumed, rather than the body, as in celiac disease. Food intolerance reactions are digestive system responses. Neither food allergies nor food intolerances cause permanent damage to the body as celiac disease can. Additionally, for allergies and intolerances, the time it takes to trigger a reaction from food is seconds to minutes. In celiac disease, symptoms develop over a longer period of time.

ASK YOURSELF THIS

- *What would you do if someone told you your symptoms were "all in your head"?*

- *Before you were diagnosed with celiac disease, had you heard about the disease? What did you know about it?*

- *What are the symptoms of your celiac disease? How did you deal with them?*

- *Although having a disease can be scary and challenging, finally knowing what is going on with their bodies can be a relief to some people. What was your reaction when you first learned you had celiac disease?*

- *Has anyone ever mistaken your condition with a food allergy? How did you explain the difference between the two?*

WHY ME? CAUSES AND RISK FACTORS

Antoine hated the way his skin looked and felt. Even zits were better than this. At least they went away eventually and they didn't itch all the time. For the last few months, small blister-like sores had formed on his elbows, knees, and butt. They'd burn for a bit

Wearing long sleeves covers up your dermatitis herpetiformis, but the rash can still be uncomfortable and make focusing on schoolwork tough.

and then they'd itch like crazy. He could manage the places on his elbows and knees but he had to be sneaky about scratching elsewhere. One day he was squirming in his desk when Mrs. Nelms asked if he needed to go to the bathroom, which made the class howl with laughter. Even Ellie, the girl he liked, tried to hide a smile.

His mom had taken him to the family doctor because Antoine's constant scratching was driving her crazy too. The doctor prescribed steroid cream, which helped some but not for long. Another doctor said the rash was caused by bug bites or an allergy to laundry detergent, but Antoine and his mom knew it had to be more. They hadn't changed laundry detergent and no mosquito bite looked or itched like this.

Finally, they consulted a dermatologist. Dr. Westin numbed an area near Antoine's elbow and took a skin sample. "We'll see what this biopsy shows under the microscope," he said, "but I'm suspecting it is dermatitis herpetiformis, a manifestation of celiac disease."

"What's celiac disease?" Antoine asked.

"It's a condition in which your body cannot handle gluten," the doctor replied.

"What does that mean? Do people die from it?" Antoine wanted to know.

"It is serious, which is why we're testing. But you'll be fine as long as you remove anything with gluten from your diet."

Easy for you to say, Antoine thought as he followed his mom from the office. But what he really wanted to know was: if he had dermatitis herpetiformis, how'd he catch it in the first place?

UNKNOWN CAUSE

Many people are as confused as Antoine about celiac disease—and with good reason. It is a confusing disease with symptoms that mimic those of other diseases and conditions, and it

WHAT IS DERMATITIS HERPETIFORMIS?

Dermatitis herpetiformis (DH) is a manifestation of celiac disease that affects the skin and most often appears as an itchy, blistery rash on elbows, knees, and buttocks. Only approximately 40 percent of people with DH have positive blood tests for celiac disease, though.[1] In those with celiac disease, between 15 and 25 percent have or develop DH.[2] But DH rarely affects children or adolescents. Doctors think this is because the immune system has to be stimulated for a long time for DH to develop.

People with DH always have celiac disease, even if their intestines don't show any damage from the disease. Scientists are unsure why this is. People are most likely to develop DH between the ages of 15 and 40, but it can appear at any age.[3] Treatment for DH includes eliminating gluten from your diet and taking an oral antibiotic called Dapsone, which helps keep the rash under control. Eliminating gluten from your diet is still the best way to treat and prevent the rash.

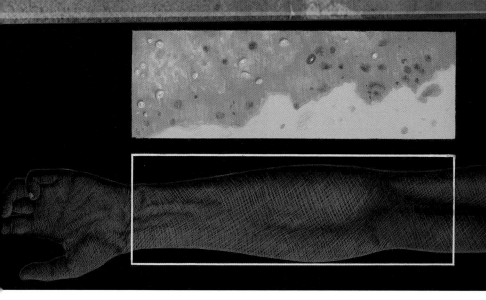

Dermatitis herpetiformis is a rash consisting of very itchy lesions and blisters.

is also confused with food allergies. The first thing to learn about celiac disease is that it is not a condition you can catch from the air or another person. That said, scientists are still not absolutely sure what causes celiac disease.

INSIDE YOUR BODY

What happens to your body when you eat gluten? Scientists do know that the disease starts in your small intestine, where most of the digestion and absorption of food happens. The small intestine is made up of three sections: the duodenum, the jejunum, and the ileum. Each section has a different job and absorbs different nutrients. Along the lining of the small intestine are millions of tiny, fingerlike structures called villi. They cover the inside of your small

MORE ABOUT YOUR SMALL INTESTINE

The small intestine is approximately 22 feet (7 m) long. Food stays in the small intestine for approximately four hours, where it is digested and absorbed into the bloodstream. The remaining food then passes into the large intestine for further digestion and absorption.

intestine, like a plush shag carpet, and allow food molecules containing nutrients to pass into your bloodstream. Then the nutrients travel throughout your body to help you grow and function at top potential. In a way, villi are responsible for you staying healthy. Without them, the nutrients from the food you eat cannot enter your bloodstream to nourish your body.

For people who do not have celiac disease, gluten is easily digested and absorbed in the small intestine. If you have celiac disease, a part of gluten called gliadin is seen as a foreign invader in the body. This triggers an inflammatory response in the villi to get rid of the "invaders." Inflammatory responses are a normal way for the body to get rid of invaders in the body, but in the case of celiac disease, constant inflammation of villi from gliadin eventually destroys the villi. Once villi are destroyed, the lining of your small intestine loses its ability to absorb the nutrients in the food you eat.

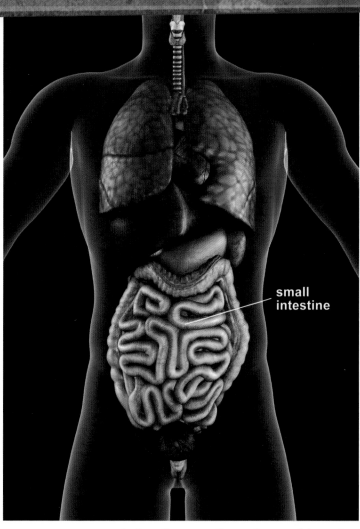

Celiac disease affects the small intestine.

The nutrients pass through your body and come out as waste material.

All three parts of the small intestine can be damaged by celiac disease—no matter what they are responsible for absorbing. But symptoms of the disease vary depending on which part of the small intestine is affected. For example, the jejunum is responsible for absorbing proteins, carbohydrates, fats, and some vitamins and minerals. A person with damage in this area may lack energy and suffer symptoms related to vitamin deficiencies. The ileum absorbs vitamin B_{12} and bile salts important in fat absorption. A person lacking vitamin B_{12} may have nerve symptoms including impaired memory or thinking.

RISK FACTORS

Scientists have identified several risk factors that increase your chances of getting celiac disease. First, celiac disease is hereditary. This means if someone in your family has celiac disease, you are more likely to develop the disease than someone who does not have a relative with the disease. Why is this? Scientists have found that approximately 95 percent of people with celiac disease have the genes HLA DQ2 or DQ8.[4]

In addition, the cleanliness of your surroundings as a baby may determine

CELIAC DISEASE BY THE NUMBERS

- In a US study, 60 percent of children and 41 percent of adults diagnosed with celiac disease had no symptoms.
- If your parent or sibling has celiac disease, you have a one in 22 chance of having it too.
- If your aunt, uncle, or cousin has celiac disease, you have a one in 39 chance of having it too.[5]

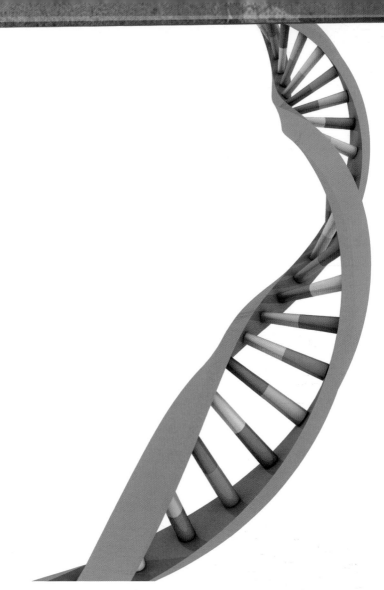

*Certain genes in DNA contribute to a higher
risk for developing celiac disease.*

how well your immune system develops.
Scientists suggest the more exposed you were
to germs as a baby, the less likely you are to
develop autoimmune diseases, such as celiac
disease, because your body has learned how

to decipher between harmful and harmless substances. Other factors that seem to trigger celiac disease are infections, surgery, or stressful events.

Finally, if you have the genes that put you at risk, gluten needs to be present in your diet. If you never eat foods such as wheat, rye, barley, and possibly oats, which contain gluten, you won't develop the disease. But in US society, that is pretty hard to do if you consume processed foods, as most contain gluten.

LEAKY GUT

If you have celiac disease, you may also have what's called a leaky gut, which is a manifestation of celiac disease. Normally, your small intestine cells are "glued" together by what are called tight junctions (tiny spaces between the cells). In leaky gut, the intestine is damaged, and particles, including but not limited to bacteria, toxins, and undigested food particles, "leak" into the circulatory system, which transports nutrients from the intestine to the liver. These particles provoke an immune response and lead to symptoms such as bloating, abdominal pain, joint pain, muscle pain, and fatigue. Leaky gut can result from any condition leading to intestinal damage, so it is not solely linked to celiac disease.

ASK YOURSELF THIS

- Do you have dermatitis herpetiformis? How do you respond if people ask you what it is?

- Do you fully understand the causes of celiac disease? Where can you go to find out more information?

- Does celiac disease run in your family? Have you had any risk factors in your life that may have led to the development of celiac disease? What are they?

- What is the hardest part for you about having celiac disease?

FROM BAD TO WORSE: COMPLICATIONS

Andrea was so tired she wanted to drop. Lately when she sat at the dinner table, all she felt like doing was laying her head on the table and sleeping. Her parents thought she was being lazy when she stayed in bed all day on weekends. And in school, dragging herself from class to class took all her effort. Sometimes she felt like she just couldn't get enough air. No matter how much she slept, she had dark circles under her eyes, and her skin was so pale she looked like a ghost. Her parents finally realized something was wrong when she didn't even feel like participating in the fun on their vacation.

When her mother took Andrea to the doctor, the doctor examined her and took blood samples. When the results came back, they showed she had a low red blood cell count, which meant she had a condition called anemia and was suffering from malnourishment. The doctor prescribed iron and other supplements and a directive to eat more nourishing foods, and sent Andrea on her way. But even though Andrea followed the doctor's orders, they didn't seem to help. Something more had to be wrong.

After several more trips to the clinic, the doctor finally ordered different blood tests and discovered Andrea had celiac disease. Soon after eliminating gluten from her diet, Andrea regained her strength. The next time they went on vacation, her parents couldn't keep up with her.

If you risk eating gluten once you're feeling better, complications can again arise.

AN ANSWER AT LAST

Andrea was glad to finally have some answers. Once she was feeling better, though, it was harder to follow the diet because she didn't feel sick. But, as her doctor kept reminding her, if she ignored her disease not only would she feel lousy again, but her small intestine would suffer more damage. She had to commit to the diet and stick with it, because it takes time for the small intestine to heal.

This difference between how a person feels and the slow rate of intestinal healing can cause problems. Some people feel so much better after not eating gluten, they think they can begin eating gluten occasionally without harm. But doing so can lead to complications. Still others may not eat gluten but still have complications due to accidental ingestion of gluten or conditions not related to celiac disease. So what are some of these conditions and complications?

LACTOSE INTOLERANCE

Lactose intolerance is caused by an inability to break down the lactose in dairy products. Lactose is a sugar found in the milk of mammals and in products made from milk, such as cheese or ice cream. Lactose can't be absorbed into the body unless it is broken down into smaller

FIVE CALCIUM-RICH FOODS OTHER THAN DAIRY

If you can't drink milk because of lactose intolerance, you'll need to get calcium from other sources. Of course, you can use the lactose-free dairy products on the market. But you can also eat some of these calcium-rich foods:

1. Leafy green vegetables, such as spinach, kale, and greens
2. Shellfish and fish, such as salmon, ocean perch, blue crab, and clams
3. Soybeans and other soy products
4. White beans and pinto beans
5. Blackstrap molasses

sugars. An enzyme called lactase, found in the small intestine, does this. If your small intestine is damaged from celiac disease, the enzymes do not work properly. But after eliminating gluten from your diet, your small intestine begins to heal, you may be better able to absorb lactose, and the intolerance may go away.

GASTROPARESIS

Another condition that might cause problems is gastroparesis. This is a condition that affects the length of time the stomach takes to empty food into the small intestine. Symptoms include feeling full before you've eaten enough, bloating, belly pain, and upset stomach.

SMALL INTESTINAL BACTERIAL OVERGROWTH

We all have bacteria living in our digestive tracts.

PROBIOTICS

Our bodies would not be able to digest food without the help of beneficial bacteria called probiotics. Approximately 400 types of good bacteria exist in the human digestive tract. The good bacteria keep the harmful ones from growing too much. Research has shown that children with celiac disease have fewer beneficial bacteria in their small and large intestines than children without celiac disease. Eating foods with probiotics, such as yogurt, will aid your intestines.

The number increases the farther down the digestive tract you go. These bacteria help us digest our food. But sometimes, the number of bacteria is too much. This condition is called small intestinal bacterial overgrowth (SIBO). Doctors can determine if you have SIBO by using sophisticated tests. SIBO is treated with probiotics that kill the overgrowth and balance your digestive system.

INFERTILITY

One way some people find out they have celiac disease is when they want to start a family. A study at Thomas Jefferson University Hospital in Philadelphia found that the rate of miscarriages and infertility is at least four times higher in people with celiac disease than in the general population.[1] Although the exact reasons aren't clear, researchers believe celiac disease can affect the health of the reproductive systems in both females and males.

OSTEOPOROSIS

If you have celiac disease, you may not be absorbing the minerals your body requires. One mineral in particular is calcium. Insufficient calcium can lead to osteoporosis, which is the loss of the density and the mineral substance of the bone. Without enough calcium, your bones can break just from carrying your own body weight. Lack of calcium can also cause muscle spasms and even convulsions.

MALNUTRITION

Malabsorption may lead to malnutrition because your body cannot absorb foods' nutrients. Instead of being absorbed, nutrients are passed through your body as waste. Your body may not get enough vitamins and minerals such as folate, folic acid, iron, vitamin D, or vitamin B_{12}, which can lead to delay in development and growth. Signs of malnutrition are weight loss, fatigue, and dizziness.

CANCER

Although frightening to think about, it is true that having celiac disease raises a person's risk of developing cancer. The risk increases the longer a person remains undiagnosed with celiac disease

WHAT'S THE BIG DEAL ABOUT OATS?

Since oats are a relative of wheat, rye, and barley, there is a question as to whether they are safe for people with celiac disease to eat. Until now, doctors counseled against eating oats. But recently, the consumption of pure oats (those that contain no other gluten-containing products) has been tested and found acceptable. However, some highly sensitive celiac disease patients may still have a reaction and should not add oats to their diets.

If you have celiac disease, chronic dizziness may be a sign you are malnourished.

or if a person with the disease still eats gluten. Andrea's risk is low because her celiac disease was diagnosed as a teenager and she has eliminated gluten from her diet.

One of the reasons scientists think the risk increases is that since the immune system is negatively affected it may not be as able to fight cancer cells. Also, the fact that your small intestine has been damaged makes it more prone to absorbing things it shouldn't, such as cancer-causing agents. In addition, the same intestine damage makes it harder for your body to absorb cancer-fighting substances. Finally, the fact that celiac disease causes inflammation of tissues makes them more susceptible to becoming cancerous.

SEEK HELP

After your celiac diagnosis, staying in regular contact with your doctor is the best way to cope with any complications you may experience. Your doctor will likely order regular tests to assess how well you are healing.

TIPS FOR TAKING IRON

If your body cannot absorb iron, a complication can be anemia. If you have to take additional iron because of anemia caused by celiac disease, keep these tips in mind:

- The body absorbs iron better when you take it with a source of vitamin C such as orange juice.
- Iron supplements don't work as well when taken with food.
- Don't take iron supplements at the same time as antacids.
- Iron supplements may be taken with food to prevent intestinal upset.

ASK YOURSELF THIS

- *Have you ever had complications from celiac disease? What were they? How did you deal with them?*

- *Why isn't it safe to eat gluten even when your symptoms disappear?*

- *What if you are not eating gluten and are still having intestinal problems? What can you do?*

- *What can you do if you're worried about complications from celiac disease?*

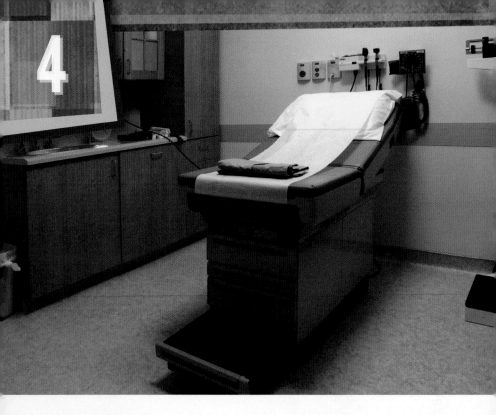

I HAVE WHAT? TESTS AND DIAGNOSIS

Roberto raked the pile of books off his desk onto the floor. "I don't care what you say, Mom!" he yelled. "Dr. Blake can stuff it. I don't feel sick. Why should I take the tests?" That's what happened a year ago when Roberto and his mom returned from the doctor's

A doctor's visit is required to accurately diagnose celiac disease.

office. They'd learned that Roberto's delayed growth might be the result of celiac disease, but he'd have to be tested to find out for sure.

Roberto had stalled about going to the doctor for as long as he could. "It's no big deal," he had told his mom when she'd expressed concern about the fact that he wasn't growing. It became a problem for Roberto, though, when his younger brother, Uziel, shot up and was suddenly towering over him.

But Roberto would rather stay small than be tested. From what Dr. Blake said, blood would be drawn for the tests—that meant needles, and there was nothing Roberto hated more than needles. Then there was something called an endoscopy, which involved snooping around in his intestines and taking bits to study under a microscope. Sick! Was it all worth becoming a walking science experiment just to find out he'd have to be on a special diet the rest of his life? No way. But Roberto finally gave in when kids at school started teasing him.

The only good thing about the whole situation was that if the tests proved Roberto had celiac disease, Uziel would have to have tests too. And Uziel was even more afraid of needles than he was.

A TRICKY DISEASE

Celiac disease is tricky to diagnose. One reason for this is because many people don't experience the classic symptoms of the disease—diarrhea, bloating, and upset stomach. Symptoms vary widely from person to person and can mimic those of other medical issues, possibly leading to a false diagnosis—or at least one that does not get to the root of the problem. You might have achy muscles and joints that your doctor may diagnose as growing pains. You may just have symptoms of a skin rash. Or, there may not be any noticeable symptoms at all. Most adults don't discover they have

CELEBRITY WITH CELIAC DISEASE

Elisabeth Hasselbeck, cohost on *The View*, finally got a celiac disease diagnosis after ten years of trying to find out what was wrong with her. Hasselbeck's problems began in college when she ended up in the hospital after a three-week trip to Central America. The doctor said she'd picked up a bacterial infection. Afterward, she was hungry all the time but the only foods she felt like eating were soft-serve ice cream and rice cereal. When she was a contestant on the television show *Survivor* and had very little to eat, she felt better than she had in years because she wasn't eating any forms of gluten. When she returned to the United States, though, she ate a regular diet and suffered from the same stomach pain, diarrhea, and bloated belly as before. In the next years she was diagnosed with irritable bowel syndrome, but finally, in 2002, she diagnosed herself with celiac disease. A doctor later confirmed this diagnosis. Hasselbeck's story illustrates how tricky a celiac disease diagnosis can be.

Although being diagnosed with celiac disease is the first step to feeling better, you may still feel overwhelmed and upset, and that's okay.

celiac disease for four to nine years after first developing it. And, it may take as many as eight doctor visits for children to be diagnosed.

WHEN TESTS ARE A GOOD THING

You may have shared or currently share Roberto's reluctance to be tested, but despite the inconvenience and possible discomfort, the tests can be good things. Sure, you may have had your share of tests already and not gotten any answers about why you've been sick, but, as you've read, diagnosing celiac disease can

PREPARING FOR MEDICAL TESTS

How you prepare for your tests can affect the results. Ask your doctor if you have any questions concerning your tests. Here are some tips that may make the process easier and more productive:

- **Continue eating a diet containing gluten until blood tests have been taken.**
- **Fast for eight hours before your endoscopy.**
- **Before your endoscopy, check with the doctor about any medicines you are currently taking.**
- **Ask a family member to go with you.**

take a long time for most people. Still, the tests may give you answers about your body's reactions— and a course of action to treat the disease.

If you haven't been sick and are undergoing tests because someone is making you, take some deep breaths and try to understand that the person is only trying to help you. If the tests for celiac disease are negative, there is no harm done. If the tests confirm you have celiac disease or are at risk for developing it in the future, knowing that information now may prevent complications of the disease. And just think, for once, these are tests you don't have to study for!

Before going to the doctor, write down all symptoms, foods eaten, and other information you don't want to forget to discuss.

PREPARATION

You'll want to be fully prepared when you go to the doctor. Have your complete medical history ready. This doesn't mean you have to remember every time you scraped your knees, but you will need to tell the doctor the larger medical events in your life, including all possible symptoms you've experienced and when they began.

Keep a journal of symptoms and the foods you ate around the time the symptoms started. Be sure to include all the details, including the gross ones that you might be embarrassed about. Just remember, you aren't the first person to tell a doctor about diarrhea and excessive gas, and you won't be the last. The more information you can give your doctor, the better informed he or she will be about your symptoms, which will help in deciding what tests to give you.

It is also important not to eliminate gluten from your diet two to six weeks before you've been tested. Without gluten in your system, your test results may be negative for celiac disease. This could delay your diagnosis and put you at risk for even more small intestine damage if you have celiac disease.

EXAMINATION

After the doctor gets your history, it is time for a physical exam. Yes, you'll probably have to wear one of those flimsy paper gowns, and it might be a little embarrassing, but, hey, just remember you don't have anything the doctor hasn't seen before and it's not an all-day deal. It will probably take ten minutes, then you'll be back in your jeans and T-shirt!

What is the purpose of a physical exam? The doctor needs to measure your blood

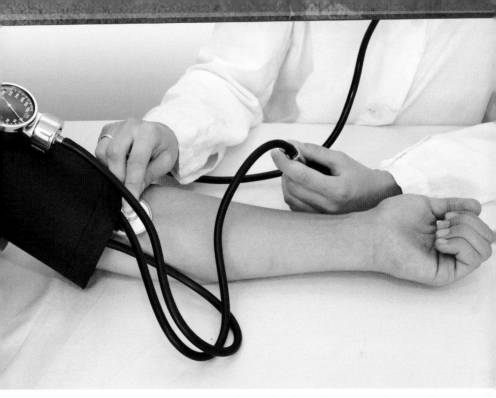

Checking blood pressure is a routine task during your physical exam.

pressure, pulse, height, and weight, and listen to your heart. The doctor will also examine your skin, arms, legs, and mouth. Next, the doctor will examine your belly to look for any painful or enlarged areas. He or she may even need to do a rectal exam, which is a procedure where the doctor inserts a gloved, lubricated finger of one hand into the rectum. The doctor uses the other hand to press on the lower belly to check for tenderness, growths, hard areas, or enlargements. After performing the exam, the doctor may take a stool sample by placing feces on the glove into a container for laboratory examination. This may be necessary to determine some digestive problems.

BLOOD WORK

Currently, one of the ways people are tested for celiac disease is through blood analysis. The most important blood test you will have if celiac disease is suspected will be the tissue transglutaminase (tTG) IgA test. A protein called tTG is found in most of your body's tissues. If you have celiac disease, antibodies that your body produced to fight against that particular protein will be present in your blood. Antibodies are proteins created to fight something attacking your immune system. But the doctor will order another test to confirm your celiac disease diagnosis because the same antibodies can be present with other diseases such as heart and liver failure.

The doctor may order an endomysial antibody (EMA) test to make sure the results of the tTG IgA test for celiac disease are correct. EMA goes after the same protein as tTG. If you have both EMA and tTG in your blood then the doctor knows for sure you have celiac disease.

Blood tests are not 100 percent accurate. In fact, they can come up negative for various reasons, such as if you haven't been consuming gluten for a while or if you have another condition, such as heart or liver disease, which

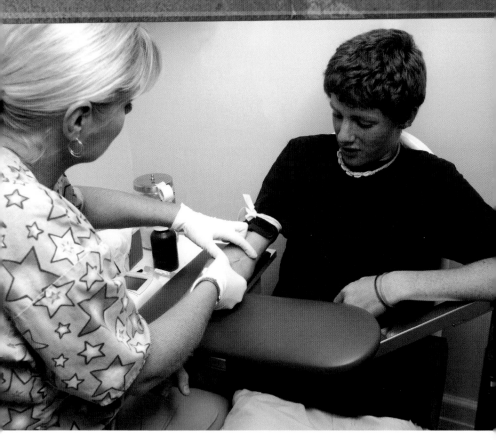

Your blood will be drawn and tested to determine if you have celiac disease.

can cause false results. This may delay your celiac disease diagnosis.

GENETIC TESTING

In addition, a doctor may order genetic testing if the blood tests aren't conclusive or if someone else in the family is sick and suspected of having celiac disease. In that case, the doctor checks to see if the HLA DQ2 or DQ8 are present in your blood, since celiac disease can run in families. Remember, if you have one of the genes, it does not necessarily mean you have or will develop celiac disease.

ENDOSCOPY

After blood tests indicate you may have celiac disease, your doctor will recommend an endoscopy. Also called an EGD, an endoscopy takes a biopsy of your small intestine. It is an outpatient procedure, which means you can leave the hospital or a special clinic soon after it is done. A tube-shaped instrument, which is about as big around as your little finger, is passed down your throat and into the duodenum of your small intestine. The tube contains a tiny camera, which takes pictures of the intestinal wall. Then, the doctor passes flexible forceps that look like tiny tweezers down the tube in your throat. Tiny snips of your intestinal tissue are taken and sent to a pathologist, who examines them for damage.

CAPSULE ENDOSCOPY

Sometimes, if a doctor suspects you have celiac disease in a far-reaching part of your intestine, he or she might order a capsule endoscopy. For this test, you swallow a vitamin-sized camera that takes a video as it passes through your digestive tract. The pictures are transmitted to a recorder on a belt you wear for eight hours. When the test is over, you remove the belt and the images are downloaded onto a computer for the doctor to analyze. The capsule passes out of your body in a bowel movement and can be flushed down the toilet.

Once test results come back, your doctor will discuss your diagnosis and the next steps you should take.

The biopsy doesn't hurt because you don't have nerve endings in your intestine. The only thing you may have is a slightly sore throat from the endoscope rubbing against it. The whole test takes only approximately ten to 15 minutes. If you really want to, you can probably be back to school in time to take more tests—the math or English kind!

DIAGNOSIS

When your test results come back positive, you will need to start making changes in your life to treat your condition. Your doctor will want to continue monitoring your health as he or she searches for answers and ways to help you feel better. Although the disease has no cure, you are lucky to be diagnosed when you are young. The longer celiac disease is left untreated, the more likely you are to develop complications

SIX COMMON QUESTIONS AND ANSWERS

1. **Does an endoscopy hurt?**
   No, you are given medicine to make you sleepy and the back of the throat is numbed so you can't feel the tube passing down it.
2. **Will I feel it when the biopsies are taken?**
   No, your small intestine has no nerve endings so you won't feel the snip.
3. **What do the pictures of my small intestine show?**
   The pictures show the condition of the villi lining your small intestine.
4. **If I have celiac disease, can I eat gluten on special occasions?**
   No, it is not safe to eat gluten at any time.
5. **Should I take vitamins and what kind should I take?**
   You should take vitamins and minerals under the direction of your doctor or dietician.
6. **How often will I have to have checkups for my celiac disease?**
   The number of checkups will depend on how sick you were when you were diagnosed and if you have related conditions the doctor wants to monitor. But usually, you will have yearly physicals and tests.

due to your inability to absorb nutrients. The earlier you are diagnosed, the earlier you can start changing your diet and lifestyle to prevent long-term health conditions and related autoimmune diseases.

ASK YOURSELF THIS

- *What tests have you undergone to diagnose your celiac disease? What was your experience with them?*

- *What do you wish someone would invent to make testing for celiac disease easier?*

- *Did you have to continue eating gluten before getting tested? Was this difficult? Why or why not?*

- *What are some advantages and disadvantages of knowing that you definitely have celiac disease?*

- *Do you have more questions about testing and diagnosis? How can you find out more?*

- *How long ago did you get your diagnosis? How did you feel when you first heard the doctor tell you that you have celiac disease?*

LIFE WITHOUT GLUTEN: TREATMENT

Jason scanned the food list the dietician had just handed him. He'd only been sitting in her office five minutes and already he knew her goal was to starve him. He slapped the paper back on her desk, slumping back into his chair. Gluten was in everything, even things that weren't food!

"Jason, you can still have many of your favorite foods," his mom said, pointing to the apples and carrots at the top of the list.

"Oh sure," Jason shot back. "Just call me a rabbit." He could almost hear the guys at school if he started lugging carrots, celery sticks, and apples in his lunch every day. They'd laugh him off the face of the earth.

"Look, Jas," Jason's dad said a couple of weeks later while shooting baskets on the driveway. "Seems to me following that diet is doing wonders for your shot. You're already running rings around me. Think of how awesome your shot will be when you're completely healed!"

Jason had to agree. After he'd calmed down a bit, he realized he was already feeling better, and he had to admit his mom was really working hard to make meals taste good. She was showing him he could substitute normal food with gluten-free, or GF, foods. Last Friday he had friends over for a barbecue and everyone had burgers. After they'd taken their first bites, Jason revealed the truth. It was great to see the surprised looks on his friends' faces. They all said the buns didn't taste different.

"Of course, you get six starved 14-year-olds at a dining table and they'll eat anything that isn't nailed down," his dad said, but Jason knew he was only teasing. Eating GF foods wasn't bad once you got used to it. And at least he didn't have a killer gut ache around the clock anymore.

A GF DIET

If there's anything good about having celiac disease, it is that you don't have to take medicines or undergo painful treatments to control it. Treatment doesn't involve shots or surgery. For most people, the only treatment they need is to follow a gluten-free diet. Following a GF diet removes the source of irritation from the small intestine, allowing the

GRAINS TO AVOID

You almost have to be a detective to tell which grains and grain products are safe to eat when you have celiac disease. Stay away from a product if the label includes any of the following words or terms: barley, bran, bromated flour, bulgur, couscous, cracked wheat, durum flour, einkorn, emmer, enriched flour, farina, faro, graham flour, hydrolyzed wheat protein, kamut, matzo flour/meal, phosphated flour, plain flour, rye, self-rising flour, semolina, spelt, triticale, wheat bran, wheat germ, wheat protein, wheat starch, or white flour. People with celiac disease can tolerate small amounts of oats, but it is best to choose GF varieties due to possible cross-contamination in grain-handling facilities.

villi time to heal. The rate at which an individual starts feeling better after beginning a GF diet varies. It depends on how long the person has had the disease and the severity of the small intestine's damage. Some people respond in weeks, while others continue experiencing symptoms for a lifetime. How well a person adheres to the diet and the age at which a person is diagnosed can make a difference. Younger people heal more quickly than adults.

How will you eat safely when so many foods contain gluten? Gone are the days of grabbing bags of nacho-flavored whatever off store shelves, tossing them into the grocery cart, and going home to enjoy. From now on, you must analyze everything you come in contact with, and you must learn to plan ahead.

LEARNING ABOUT FOOD

The first step to a GF diet is education. Learn what foods contain gluten and how to look for hidden gluten in items. When you first look at the limitations of a GF diet, it might be frightening. *Fresh* and *plain* are words to remember when shopping for GF foods. Fresh foods are naturally your best nutritional sources. Many foods are naturally gluten-free, such as fruits, vegetables, beef, pork, poultry, fish, nuts, beans, and eggs. These should be among

FLOUR YOU CAN EAT

Many different kinds of flour are used to make GF products. An Internet search will yield cookbooks and recipes for using these flours to make your own GF goods. The following are flours you can use: almond, amaranth, arrowroot, bean, buckwheat, corn, flax, millet, nut, potato, quinoa, rice, sorghum, soy, tapioca, teff, and gluten-free oat.

your first choices for eating.

Also, a good rule of thumb is to avoid packaged and processed foods. Generally, highly processed foods are not as healthy as unprocessed foods. But they also pose a greater risk of containing gluten due to cross-contamination. If you want extras, such as sauces or dressings, it is best to add your own GF trimmings.

You may rely on "safe" foods at first—just the ones that you know won't make you sick. But there is such a wide variety of safe foods; limiting your choices out of fear isn't necessary. The American Dietetic Association (ADA) offers suggestions for staying healthy on a GF diet. First, the ADA suggests finding a registered dietician to help you sort out what you can and cannot eat. If your doctor doesn't recommend someone, check with a local celiac disease support group or contact hospitals in the area to see if they have a celiac disease clinic or a dietician on staff who is knowledgeable about

Gluten-free grains such as quinoa are nutritional and can be used to make tasty dishes.

the disease. Not only can the dietician help with the GF choices, he or she can also make sure the choices you make allow you to get all the nutrients you need.

Next, the ADA suggests finding out about alternative grains. Although it may seem like it at first, wheat isn't the only grain that's available. Many more grains are available that taste great and are filled with nutrients. If you don't see what you need at your local grocery store, talk to the manager and ask that the store stock some of your favorites.

LABEL READING 101

The ADA also says to learn about the ingredients in foods. Many products contain hidden sources of gluten. Even foods such as soy sauce can contain gluten, so it's important to learn how to read food labels. Also, keep an eye out for the GF label on products. It is important, however, not to confuse that with "wheat-free." Wheat-free foods can still contain gluten.

Be sure to check the labels on spices, sauces, and toppings before using them. Some spices contain flours as carriers to help the spices flow out of their packages more smoothly. Sauces, sprays, and toppings can contain food starch, which can contain gluten.

Reading food labels can be intimidating at first. But knowing a few things to look for will help. You need to watch out for the following ingredients and terms when

LABELING LAWS

In 2006, the US Congress implemented the Food Allergen Labeling and Consumer Act (FALCA). This law made it mandatory for companies to label their products if they contained these eight allergy-causing foods: eggs, milk, peanuts, tree nuts (pistachio nuts, walnuts, pine nuts, pecans, macadamia nuts, cashews, hazelnuts, Brazil nuts, almonds), fish, shellfish, soybeans, and wheat. Although it was supposed to be law by 2008, a GF label has still not been implemented.

Reading food labels will become an integral part of your treatment.

examining a label: brewer's yeast, modified food starch, dextrin, and malt (which comes from barley). Modified food starch could contain wheat. But it is safe if it is identified as tapioca, potato, rice, or cornstarch. Always check soy sauce to be sure it is GF. If it isn't identified as such, don't use it.

When you do eat packaged food, you need to read labels carefully. Laws in the United States and Canada require food manufacturers to label whether products are GF. Even if you ate a certain packaged food before, you still need to check the label again. Companies change their labels and product ingredients all the time. If you are concerned or confused about an ingredient, contact the manufacturer and ask if the food contains gluten. In other words, when in doubt, find out.

COOKING

One of the best ways to guarantee your food isn't contaminated with gluten is to cook it

DRAWBACKS TO EATING GLUTEN-FREE

Temptation: Giving up something is difficult. Changing your diet is no exception. You will have times when your resistance is low and you will be tempted to eat foods with gluten, during holidays for example. To help keep you from slipping, remember how consuming gluten makes you feel and always have GF snacks with you.

Pressure: Be prepared with reasons to explain why you can't eat a certain food. That way you won't cave under pressure to eat foods you shouldn't. Ahead of time, ask a friend or family member to come to defend your food choices, if necessary.

Expense: According to one study, GF food usually costs approximately 240 percent more than conventional foods.[1] This is a big drawback for many people. If the cost of packaged GF foods is too expensive, cooking your own food from naturally GF fresh foods might be a good option.

yourself. If you don't know how, ask your parent or another adult to teach you. Then keep practicing. And don't be afraid to experiment. Whatever experience you gain now will come in handy when you are on your own.

A helpful practice is to plan meals and snacks ahead of time. Make meal planning, preparation, and grocery shopping family tasks. That way everyone is involved in your GF efforts and you won't feel so isolated. You may find a greater variety of GF foods online. You might also find it cheaper to order in bulk.

MORE THAN FOOD

Label reading doesn't stop with food. Other products can contain gluten and can pose a risk too. Gluten cannot be absorbed through the skin, but there is still a risk that gluten in some products will be ingested. You'll need to check cosmetics, such as lipstick and lip balm, for gluten. You might be contaminated if you lick your lips and swallow some.

Ask your doctor or pharmacist about any prescription drugs you take. The law that requires manufacturers to list allergens in food does not apply to medicine. It's possible your medications could contain gluten. The same goes with any vitamins or supplements you take, though you can check for GF labels on the products before you purchase them. Be sure to check the labels on name brand and generic medication. Ask your pharmacist or doctor if you have questions. The following list might indicate the product contains gluten, especially if the source is not specified: pregelatinized starch, dextrates, dextrimaltose, caramel coloring, and dextrin.

REPLACING NUTRIENTS

One thing to keep in mind is that since you are no longer eating foods containing gluten, you are missing out on some important nutrients; therefore, it is important to eat a variety of other healthy foods. But you may still need to take multivitamins or other supplements. Calcium, folate, vitamin D, iron, and B_{12} are the vitamins and minerals that may be deficient in your body. Your doctor or dietician can advise you about what to take.

RECIPES FOR IMPROVEMENT

You will continue to see improvements in GF foods at the grocery store and elsewhere. Just look at the efforts of food chemists Scott Bean and Tilman Schober from the Grain Quality and Structure Research Unit in Manhattan, Kansas. They are working on a problem that has plagued GF bakers—using an alternative flour to

Learning to cook a few recipes will allow you greater freedom and responsibility in the management of your disease.

make bread that better matches wheat bread's qualities. As yet, nothing quite measures up to gluten for making bread rise and taste flavorful. But Bean and Schober have removed fat from corn, which creates a flour that makes bread dough rise better and have an elastic nature closer to wheat bread. Eventually, they hope to make bread from a type of grain called sorghum that will be a fluffy, light replacement to regular bread.

GROWING AWARENESS, MORE CHOICES

Thankfully, as awareness about celiac disease grows, GF foods are becoming easier to find. As manufacturers see the economic advantages of the growing interest, they are making sure to prominently display GF labels on their foods. This makes them easier for you to find. They are also creating more GF alternatives to gluten-containing foods. The number of GF products is increasing by 28 percent a year.[2] You can even find GF bakeries and restaurants in larger cities, and shopping for GF groceries online is easier than ever.

OLYMPIAN WITH CELIAC DISEASE

Amy Begley is a world-class distance runner and a six-time national champion in long-distance events. But for a while, recurrent health problems kept interfering with her dreams of becoming a competitive runner. In 1999, she was diagnosed with lactose intolerance. But though she gave up dairy products, she was still plagued with intestinal problems. Finally in 2006, she was diagnosed with celiac disease. When she changed to a gluten-free diet, her digestive issues stopped. But it wasn't easy. "I'm a runner foodie. I love to eat," Begley said. "So that definitely presented some challenges."[3] But her new eating regime allowed her to have ice cream again and to compete and succeed in the 10,000-meter race in the 2008 Beijing Olympics.

Your GF diet will take some getting used to, but with practice, patience, and support, you'll adapt to your new lifestyle soon.

ASK YOURSELF THIS

- *Why do you think it is necessary to find a dietician who is familiar with celiac disease?*

- *What other drawbacks might there be to going gluten-free?*

- *What do you think the hardest part about going on a GF diet will be for you?*

- *What is the best piece of advice you've heard or read so far about eating GF foods?*

MAKING CHANGES AT HOME

"You're home!" Khalil said as Amal tossed his backpack on the bench beside the front door. "Come see what I made!"

Amal couldn't help but smile at Khalil's excitement as he followed him into the kitchen.

It may surprise you that you can still eat many foods you used to—such as chocolate cake and other treats—by using GF substitutes in the ingredients.

"Wow!" he said, when his little brother pointed to a frosted chocolate cake on the counter. His mouth watered at the sweet smell of chocolate in the air. But inside he was disappointed. Lately, Khalil had been on this cooking kick, and Mom had been letting him experiment. But chocolate cake had always been Amal's favorite. *Why didn't Mom have Khalil make coconut—a flavor Amal didn't like?* Then it wouldn't bug him not to have any!

At least he was feeling better. Only a month ago the results of his biopsy confirmed he had celiac disease. It had been a struggle adjusting to the GF diet. The first weekend after the diagnosis, Khalil and his mom had rearranged the kitchen to make it gluten-free. Now he had a cabinet just for storing his GF food plus his own colander, toaster, and cutting board. But Amal still missed regular foods. Especially chocolate cake!

"What's the occasion?" Amal asked, nodding toward the cake.

"It was my idea!" Khalil exclaimed, pushing a candle into the cake and lighting it. "You're one month gluten-free, so I made you a gluten-free cake!"

For a moment, Amal was too surprised to reply. "Well, let's dig in!" he said.

SAY HELLO TO YOUR GF KITCHEN

Families must make sacrifices when a family member is diagnosed with celiac disease. But as Amal noted, it is worth it when the family member begins feeling better. When the family member is a child or has special needs, it often falls to others to initiate and enforce gluten-free changes.

Since the kitchen is ground zero for food preparation, it will be the scene of the most adaptations to the gluten-free way of life. But that doesn't mean you need to throw everything out and start over. A few changes will bring your kitchen up to gluten-free code in no time.

CRUMBS AND CONTAMINATION

To meet your goal of establishing a safe cooking area, you must keep two c's in mind: contamination and crumbs. It only takes about one-eighth of a teaspoon of flour to cause a

"I became gluten-ly challenged at the age of four, so my struggle with the celiac diet began a lot earlier than most. . . . I just felt like a mutant freak because I couldn't eat pizza along with the other kids for a special event. It got better though. . . . Really, if you want to make being a celiac patient livable, you need to tell your friends and their parents. Just explain it as it's like being lactose intolerant, just with gluten. Just own up to it, and don't worry about looking like a dork. Eat your rice bread sandwich on the bus and enjoy it."[1]

—*Karyn James, celiac disease patient*

negative impact in a person with celiac disease, and some people are even more sensitive.[2] With that in mind, take a tour of your kitchen and check out just how crumby it actually is. There's a good chance there are some crumbs, even if your kitchen is very clean.

SEPARATE STORAGE

Creating separate storage for your GF food is important. First, think about the storage space you have available in your cabinets, pantry, refrigerator, and freezer. Divide the spaces to eliminate the possibility of contamination and dedicate one to your GF products. You might even want to label them and the storage space as such so there's no reason for confusion. For example, one freezer shelf can be dedicated to GF frozen foods. The same goes with the pantry and cabinets. Next, focus on your utensils. It's not necessary to buy separate utensils for the most part, but you will need to pay attention when you're cooking and eating. For example, don't stir your rice with the same spoon you used to stir the gravy.

Buy separate jars of anything you would put a knife into such as mayonnaise, mustard, and jelly. Label them gluten-free and be sure to explain to all family members they are gluten-free and are not to be used by everyone. If products are not kept in their original packaging,

Store all your GF food in separate containers and label them.

be sure to put "GF" labels on the containers. Even if these items are stored in separate areas, things can be misplaced.

You will also want to buy a GF-dedicated colander and cutting board. Gluten can stick in the holes of the colander and the grooves of a cutting board no matter how careful you are, so it's best to use different ones for GF food preparation.

LOCATION, LOCATION, LOCATION!

It may seem like a little detail, but thinking about where things are and what you are near while you are cooking could mean the difference between being healthy and spending three days in bed. For example, avoid passing gluten-containing foods over your GF foods. Gluten-y water from spaghetti can drip into your GF spaghetti and contaminate it. Also, prepare your GF products before cooking the ones containing gluten. It will help prevent accidental contamination.

APPLIANCES

You may want to purchase your own toaster for your GF breads if your toaster does not have removable racks. There is significant risk that your food will come in contact with crumbs if you use the family toaster. If the toaster's racks can be removed, be sure to wash them each time before using the toaster. If you

TIPS FOR GF COOKING

1. Use sunflowers seeds or crumbled rice crackers on salads instead of croutons.
2. Use cornstarch to thicken gravy, sauces, and puddings.
3. Use GF bread scraps to make bread crumbs, stuffing, or bread pudding.
4. Make sure cooking utensils and pans are cleaned thoroughly before cooking GF dishes.

If you eat toast a lot, having a separate GF toaster is a good idea.

bake your own bread, it might be worthwhile to purchase a dedicated GF bread machine. It might also be wise to label and keep your appliances in a different area from those for general use.

ASK YOURSELF THIS

- *Do you think keeping GF foods separate from other foods will be difficult? Why?*

- *What is the best way to help everyone remember the rules for a GF kitchen?*

- *What do you think would be the biggest obstacle in getting your family to make the switch to a GF kitchen? What changes would you have to make?*

- *How would you handle the situation if you found out a sibling or parent used your GF kitchenware for gluten-containing foods?*

"It's just food. If I stay true to the life-style choice of being gluten free (it is not a diet—but a decision to eat foods that don't make me sick), I feel great."[3]

—*Cameron Stevens, celiac disease patient*

NAVIGATING IN A GLUTEN-FILLED WORLD

Faith's stomach dropped. Mrs. Francis had just announced to the class that Faith's citizenship essay had been one of ten chosen in the whole state and all the winners would be taking a trip to Washington DC. Faith felt more dread than excitement. If she went,

You might be concerned that you can't take a school trip or spend time away from home, but that's not true. Being prepared will allow you to live a normal life.

it would be the first time Faith would travel without her family since she'd been diagnosed with celiac disease. How would she manage? And would the other kids think she was being a pain if she had to ask for special service at restaurants? Her mother usually asked to speak to the chef wherever they went so Faith never had to worry about it. But now she'd have to do it herself and she didn't know if she could. She never liked to call attention to herself, but since her diagnosis that seemed to be the name of the game.

The kids at her school were understanding— mostly. Her friends kept an eye on her when they went out and had even been known to grab something out of her hand if they thought it contained gluten. Most of the time they were wrong, but it was the thought that counted. But she wouldn't know any of the kids on this trip, and she didn't want to make a scene.

Maybe she'd just tell Mrs. Francis she couldn't go. Having the honor of winning was enough, she told herself. But she knew it wasn't. She could tell everybody the reason she wasn't going on the trip was because her mom needed her to babysit. Nobody would probably care anyway. But she hated to pass up the chance. She'd always wanted to see the Smithsonian and the Lincoln Memorial. Maybe if she talked to Mrs. Francis, they could figure something out together.

OUT AND ABOUT

Just when you get the hang of eating gluten-free at home, someone suggests eating out. Or someone has a birthday party and wants you to come. Or you have to go to an out-of-town speech tournament. But staying gluten-free is possible away from home. It just takes some planning and preparation for the unexpected.

At school events, there's always the option of bringing a meal. Make sure to clear it with your teacher or other school staff. Then pack a meal and enough GF snacks. That way you won't feel left out when everyone is eating on the bus. You could even pack extra snacks in case anyone wants to try GF fare.

"At this point in my life, when I'm asked why I am eating something different, it is my friends who jump up and are eager to show off their knowledge and explain exactly what being a celiac means. Honestly, would you care if one of your friends couldn't eat peanuts or something else? Of course not. Let's face it, there are a lot worse conditions out there than not being able to eat certain types of bread. Don't let celiac disease control your life, but rather take it in your stride and learn to accept that it's just part of who you are. And after all, it's just food."[1]

—Marina Keegan, celiac disease patient

Bring your own lunch to school to ensure you don't eat any gluten.

AT SCHOOL

You may worry that you can't eat with the other kids in the cafeteria, but you definitely can. Just pack your own lunches. When it comes to using snack machines, it may just be best to avoid them. Instead, bring your own GF snacks. Check with school officials to be sure it isn't against school policy. If you do decide to bring your own lunches and snacks, allow enough time in your day to prepare them. Also, let your parents know when you are about to run out of supplies.

You may wonder what will the other kids say if you're eating different food. Will they tease you? The answer is: maybe. But don't let it get you down. People tend to be afraid of and react negatively to things they don't understand. The best way to prevent this is to make sure everyone is informed. Some students will work with a teacher or the school nurse to arrange a meeting or a party to tell their classmates about their condition and answer any questions they may have. If that's not your style, print out some information sheets from one of the celiac disease Web sites and distribute them if people ask questions. Also, think of some positive responses ahead of time. In the moment you won't be at a loss for words and can defuse the situation if teasing happens.

QUESTIONS TO ASK AT A RESTAURANT

1. How do you prepare your (insert name of specific dish)?
2. Are the fries cooked in the same oil as breaded items?
3. Are the meats marinated?
4. Are the tortillas made from 100 percent corn?
5. Do you use cornstarch to thicken the gravies and sauces?

IN RESTAURANTS

There is nothing to keep you from eating at a restaurant—you just need to be prepared. In recent years, more and more restaurants started seeing the necessity of offering GF choices. Learn what those choices are and if you have a say in the choice of restaurants, suggest one that has GF options on the menu.

If you must go to a restaurant not known for being GF friendly, don't be afraid to ask questions and tell a server your special requirements. If you don't want to make a scene and you know where you are going ahead of time, call the restaurant during a less busy time and ask to speak to the chef. Then you can ask questions and make arrangements for your GF meal. Another way to get what you need is to say you're allergic to gluten. Of course, celiac disease is an autoimmune disease, not an allergy, but that's harder to explain and more people are aware of the seriousness of food allergies.

GF REQUESTS

You can give a card to your server that explains your condition and how your food needs to be prepared. The card gives the server and the chef the information they need to serve you safely, which saves you from having to explain your needs to them. You can buy these cards or print your own from Web sites about celiac disease.

If a dish containing gluten comes out to you at a restaurant, take steps to make sure the item isn't just removed and brought back to you. There could be traces of gluten on your food still. If a salad comes to you with croutons, douse it with dressing so servers can't remove the croutons and bring back the same salad. Then politely ask the server for another salad without croutons. If your hamburger mistakenly comes with a bun, cut the burger up and ask for a naked replacement. Again, be polite and don't feel guilty. You deserve a meal that will not make you sick, especially when you already asked for it and explained your case.

Ask questions about restaurants on gluten-free discussion Web sites. Or check out restaurants' Internet pages. Some will have their menus available so you can plan GF choices beforehand. You can also e-mail restaurants for

WHEN OFFERED FOOD WITH GLUTEN

When asked if you'd like a food that contains gluten, you may not want to explain the ins and outs of celiac disease. Sometimes a short answer, whether polite or funny, might be a good option. Here are a few things to say when offered food with gluten:

- "Sure, if you don't mind me spending the next few days in your bathroom."
- "Sorry, I'm allergic to that food."
- "That looks great, but I think I'll pass for now."
- "Sorry, I'm stuffed. I ate before I came."

If you want to eat at a restaurant, research ahead of time and suggest a restaurant that has some GF meal options.

information and to make arrangements ahead of time.

ON A DATE

If you go on a date, you might be in another situation where you'll need to explain your food requirements. Whether you're going to a restaurant with a group or by yourselves, it's best to let the person you're going with know about your food restrictions ahead of time. If you can, suggest a few places that serve GF dishes. If you are going with a group and you find out they are going somewhere that isn't GF friendly, tell your date you'll eat beforehand and go along for a soda. Or bring snacks you can nibble on while everyone else is eating. Letting the other person know will save him or her from being surprised and possibly hurt by your choices. It will also let you focus on having a good time.

TRAVELING

Some people with celiac disease are also worried about traveling. Again, planning will make the difference between a comfortable and miserable trip. If you are flying, bring your GF food with you. Airports and airlines aren't known for their GF fare. Take along GF crackers and cheese, fresh or dried fruit, nuts, or GF granola bars. If you are traveling by car, you can take a cooler and stock it with the foods you need.

If you are traveling to see family or friends, be aware that there may be extra temptations when you arrive. Loved ones tend to want to go all out and if you have been diagnosed since they last saw you, they

"Even if you think something is gluten-free, you should always check the ingredients just in case. In a restaurant, never say 'I'm intolerant' to something. Always say 'allergic' otherwise they'll think it's ok to just throw some gluten in there."[2]

—*Christine P.,*
celiac disease patient

may be surprised and hurt that you don't eat the rocky road chocolate cake they made especially for you. But communicating your needs to family ahead of time can save their feelings and keep you from getting sick. You should not feel that you have to eat food that contains gluten just to keep from hurting someone's feelings.

ASK YOURSELF THIS

- *How do you stay gluten-free at school?*

- *What restaurants would you like to see offer GF choices? What choices would you like to see?*

- *How would you encourage your favorite restaurant to serve GF dishes?*

- *What would you do and say if a date was not understanding of your need to be gluten-free?*

- *How would you prepare for a safe and GF trip?*

I CAN DO THIS: COPING AND THE FUTURE

Mirabel was looking forward to the meeting tonight. It was great being with other kids who had celiac disease. That had been one advantage of moving to a bigger city—finally, there was a support group she could meet with face-to-face. She appreciated her online support group. They'd helped her through the many ups and downs of the disease. But it was different to actually meet other teens in person who had this disease.

Mirabel had been diagnosed with celiac disease just before her thirteenth birthday. Even though that had only been four years ago, it seemed like a lifetime. Since then she'd become pretty good at answering all the questions people asked about her disease. At one meeting, the people in her group shared the funniest questions they had been asked. Then they went on to brainstorm ways they could inform people.

That's why going to support group meetings was so great. Mirabel didn't have to explain celiac disease, because they all shared similar experiences. What a relief to get together with other teens who knew exactly what she was going through. And, she wouldn't have to worry that they'd serve refreshments she couldn't eat!

Tonight they were going to have a cookie taste testing. They were going to their leader Jeanne's house to make and rate several of the GF varieties that were now available locally and online. That's one thing they'd all noticed—there seemed to be a lot more GF products of all kinds available these days. And at least once a month, their families met at one of the many restaurants that had started offering GF choices.

Mirabel was feeling hopeful. Maybe by the time she had her own family, knowledge and products for celiac disease would be even more common. Maybe there would be a cure! Well, she could hope.

BIG CHANGES

When someone discovers they have a life-changing disease, it's natural the knowledge will trigger strong emotions. Although it might sound dramatic to you, a life change this big can trigger the grieving process, similar to what you might experience if you had a death in the family. This is because a celiac disease diagnosis means your life is changing forever, and how you lived before will no longer work. The most important things to remember are that it takes some time to come to terms with this news, and you don't have to go through the process alone.

"I can't have celiac disease," you might protest, as Roberto did. This is especially true if you don't have obvious or painful symptoms. If you feel angry, you might direct your anger at your parents, siblings, or health-care professionals, as both Roberto and Jason did. Or you might be depressed and walk around in a fog until the realization soaks in. You may wonder why you were singled out to suffer and you may ask, "Why me?" You may even try to bargain and take risks with your health—"If I can just eat real food at my sister's wedding, I promise I'll stay gluten-free the rest of my life."

It is important to remember you don't have to face these emotions alone. Talk with a parent, teacher, counselor, or another trusted adult to help you deal with these emotions. Keep in mind that asking for help is a sign of strength, not weakness, and communicating your feelings is a sign of maturity. Talking things through is a step toward helping you pave your own path for living with celiac disease.

Finally, knowledge and positive thinking are your best friends when it comes to living gluten-free. The more you learn about celiac disease, the better you'll be able to cope. And focusing

When you're feeling overwhelmed or frustrated, talk with a parent or counselor.

on what you *can* eat instead of what you can't will make the transition to living gluten-free that much easier.

REACHING OUT

When you first find out you have celiac disease, you may feel very alone. Your busy doctor might have instructed you to look on the Internet for information about the GF diet. He or she may have given you the name of a dietician to consult. But you might want to talk with someone your own age. Many celiac disease organizations and hospital celiac disease centers sponsor support groups and discussion forums on their Web sites. Many give you options for contacting someone your own age. In larger cities, you can join face-to-face groups.

Another way to interact is to look for GF camps to attend. There are camps for all ages in several locations. Sometimes scholarships are available to help with the cost of attending.

"When living with Celiac Disease, it is vital to have a support system. It's simply a matter of 1) being educated and aware, 2) educating others, 3) surrounding yourself with supportive and empathetic people. Knowing what items have gluten in them, being able to read food labels, and understanding all of that is the first step to living a successful, non-overwhelming gluten-free lifestyle. The next step is sharing this with others, your family and friends, so that they can support you in ways that are needed. Being able to share about this disease and its effects is essential. Ignorance is bliss, but knowledge is power!"[1]

—*Ruth Gonzalez, celiac disease patient*

FUND-RAISING AND A NEW WORLD RECORD

Many people with celiac disease work to raise money for celiac disease research and increase awareness of the disease. Craig Pinto, an indoor professional league football player, broke a Guinness World Record by kicking 717 40-yard (37-m) field goals in 12 hours during his Kicking 4 Celiac fund-raiser. He raised almost $5,000 for the Celiac Disease Research Center at Columbia University.

SUPPORTING OTHERS

Reaching out can help others too. If you have celiac disease, you are the perfect person to inform others about the disease. With so many people going undiagnosed, your words might be the stimulus someone needs to go to the doctor. If you are shy and don't like to speak out, use the Web sites about celiac disease that have links allowing you to share your story in writing. Some teens with celiac disease blog about their experiences, sharing recipes and advice, and you could do the same. You could also be involved in fund-raising. Many groups and individuals hold events to raise money for celiac disease research. Participate in an event or plan one yourself.

Scientists continue their research in order to find a cure for celiac disease.

PROMISING RESEARCH

The money raised goes to organizations that fund celiac disease–related research. This is important because, for so long, celiac disease was thought to be a rare disease. Why would anyone contribute money to research a

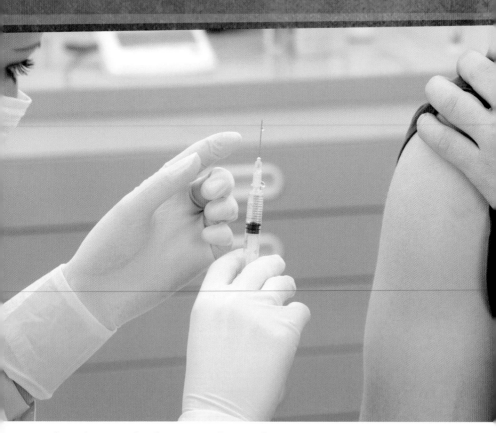

One day, vaccinations may play a role in treating celiac disease.

disease that affects so few people? But since researchers discovered celiac disease is much more common than previously thought and that it affects people in increasing numbers, contributors are more willing to step forward. Their donations are used to fund studies to find medications, explore causes, and look for cures for celiac disease.

In one current study, scientists are experimenting to perfect a vaccine people could take to keep gluten from harming them. Instead of building up your tolerance as vaccines do to bacteria, the gluten vaccine would tell your body to ignore gluten. So in the future, you might take your children in for their measles, mumps, and rubella and gluten-tolerance shots!

Other studies are testing medicines to address the leaky gut problem or to introduce enzymes that will digest the toxic parts of gluten. Still others are looking for ways to alter the immune system's response to gluten.

RESOURCES ON THE WEB

The Internet is a treasure trove of resources for teens just like you who have celiac disease. If you want to find out more information or if you're having a bad day and want to find others who know what you're going through, check out these organizations and Web sites:

- Celiac Disease Resource, www.celiacresource.org
- National Foundation for Celiac Awareness, www.celiaccentral.org
- Celiac Disease Foundation, www.celiac.org

THE BEGINNING, NOT THE END

Being diagnosed with celiac disease is not the end of the world. Sure, it will mean big changes and a lifelong commitment to a new way of eating. But you can also think of your diagnosis as the start of a healthier, more active life. After a swirl of uncertainty and confusion, you have a diagnosis. Your lifelines are the GF diet, the

Having celiac disease will not stop you from having fun, dreaming big, and reaching your goals.

growing knowledge about celiac disease, and knowing you're not alone.

ASK YOURSELF THIS

- *Do you attend any in-person or online support groups? How have these helped you? If you don't, what has stopped you from doing so?*

- *How can realizing you are not alone be helpful when dealing with celiac disease?*

- *Why do you think positive thinking is important when you have celiac disease?*

- *What are the advantages to having celiac disease?*

- *What can you do to raise awareness of celiac disease?*

JUST THE FACTS

Celiac disease is a genetic, autoimmune disease that, when gluten is consumed, causes damage to the villi lining the small intestine.

Symptoms of celiac disease vary greatly, but some classic symptoms are bloating, diarrhea, weight loss, and fatigue.

Though an estimated one in 133 people in the United States have celiac disease, 97 percent are undiagnosed.

A manifestation of celiac disease that affects the skin is dermatitis herpetiformis, which is characterized by an itchy rash on parts of the body such as the elbows and knees.

As of 2011, the only treatment for celiac disease is a GF diet.

Risk factors for developing celiac disease include having the genes that predispose you to it and the consumption of gluten.

If not treated, celiac disease can lead to other diseases and conditions such as osteoporosis, malnutrition, and cancer.

An endoscopy, which involves a biopsy of the small intestine, is often used to diagnose celiac disease.

It is imperative to learn to read food labels to determine if products contain gluten.

Those on a GF diet should not ingest foods with wheat, rye, or barley. They can, however, eat a small amount of uncontaminated oats.

Those with celiac disease need to work with a dietician to make sure they are complying with their GF diet and also meeting their nutritional needs.

Getting and giving support can help you learn to cope with celiac disease.

WHERE TO TURN

If You Suspect You Have Celiac Disease

First of all, tell your parents exactly how you've been feeling and ask if you can see a doctor. Then begin keeping a journal of everything you eat and any symptoms you may have. Go to www.celiaccentral.org/disease-symptoms-checklist/ and fill out the checklist to take with you to the doctor. At your appointment show the doctor the information you've collected and ask if you could be tested for celiac disease.

If You Are Looking for GF Products

Although more and more grocery stores are stocking GF items, not all grocery stores have those items available. Or, some just may not have the products you want. If this is the case, you can talk to the grocery store manager and request that he or she order specific products for the store. You can also visit a number of different Web sites that sell only GF products. You can find cookies, cakes, pizza dough, and more. Buy them online and have them shipped right to your home.

If You Would Like to Help a Friend Stay on the GF Diet

First, try not to be critical. As the old saying goes, put yourself in your friend's shoes. You know how difficult and discouraging it can sometimes be to stay gluten-free for life. Your friend could be tired of feeling different, especially if he or she seems to slip up more when going out with friends. Next time you plan something together, be prepared by searching online for GF selections at restaurants in the area. Or look up GF recipes online and host a cook-off at your place using GF ingredients. Ask your friend to instruct the group in cross-contamination.

If You Get the Urge to Eat Gluten Anyway

Take a minute to breathe. It can be stressful always having to pay attention to what you can and cannot eat—especially if you're the only one around you doing it. Before throwing in the towel and eating whatever you want—and getting really sick because of it—go online and find a discussion group. Or call someone from your local support group. Talking to someone who has been in your position may ease your frustrations a bit. You can vent your annoyances to that person and together try to come up with a plan for you to move forward in a positive way.

GLOSSARY

anemia
The condition of not having enough red blood cells, which is often caused by a lack of iron.

autoimmune disease
A disease in which the immune system causes the body to attack itself.

biopsy
A procedure in which a small piece of tissue is removed from the body for the purpose of being tested.

cross-contamination
When gluten-containing food, such as bread crumbs, comes into contact with gluten-free food.

dermatitis herpetiformis
A manifestation of celiac disease on the skin, characterized by an extremely itchy rash most often on the elbows, knees, and buttocks.

duodenum
The upper one-third of the small intestine.

endoscopy
A procedure in which pictures and tissue specimens are taken from the small intestine for the purpose of confirming a celiac disease diagnosis.

gluten
The sticky protein found in wheat and other foods and food-like products.

ileum

The lower one-third of the small intestine.

jejunum

The middle one-third of the small intestine.

lactose intolerance

The condition where the body does not have enough of the enzyme lactase to digest milk and other dairy products.

villi

Fingerlike protrusions on the surface of the small intestine that absorb nutrients.

ADDITIONAL RESOURCES

SELECTED BIBLIOGRAPHY

Dennis, Melinda, and Daniel A. Leffler. *Real Life With Celiac Disease: Troubleshooting and Thriving Gluten Free.* Bethesda, MD: AGA, 2010. Print.

Green, Peter H. R., and Rory Jones. *Celiac Disease: A Hidden Epidemic.* New York: William Morrow, 2010. Print.

Hasselbeck, Elisabeth. *The G-Free Diet: A Gluten-Free Survival Guide.* New York: Center Street, 2009. Print.

FURTHER READINGS

Ahern, Shauna James. *Gluten-Free Girl: How I Found the Food That Loves Me Back—& How You Can, Too.* Hoboken, NJ: Wiley, 2007. Print.

Landolphi, Robert M. *Gluten Free Every Day Cookbook: More than 100 Easy and Delicious Recipes from the Gluten-Free Chef.* Kansas City, MO: Andrews McMeel, 2009. Print.

Shepard, Jules E. Dowler. *The First Year: Celiac Disease and Living Gluten-Free: An Essential Guide for the Newly Diagnosed.* Cambridge, MA: Da Capo, 2008. Print.

Tessmer, Kimberly A. *Tell Me What to Eat If I Have Celiac Disease: Nutrition You Can Live With.* Franklin Lakes, NJ: New Page, 2009. Print.

WEB LINKS

To learn more about living with celiac disease visit ABDO
Publishing Company online at **www.abdopublishing.com**.
Web sites about living with celiac disease are featured on our
Book Links page. These links are routinely monitored and
updated to provide the most current information available.

SOURCE NOTES

CHAPTER 1. WHAT IS HAPPENING TO ME? DEFINING CELIAC DISEASE

1. "Celiac Disease Facts and Figures." *The University of Chicago Celiac Disease Center*. The University of Chicago Celiac Disease Center, 21 Aug. 2007. PDF file. 5 Jan. 2011.

2. Alessio Fasano. "Genetics and Epidemiology of Celiac Disease." n.d. PDF file. 3 June 2011.

3. "Migraine." *National Foundation for Celiac Awareness*. National Foundation for Celiac Awareness, 17 Mar. 2011. Web. 13 Jan. 2011.

CHAPTER 2. WHY ME? CAUSES AND RISK FACTORS

1. "Overview of Celiac Disease." *The University of Chicago Celiac Disease Center*. The University of Chicago Celiac Disease Center, 15 Aug. 2007. PDF file. 8 Jan. 2011.

2. Ian Blummer and Sheila Crowe. *Celiac Disease for Dummies*. Hoboken, NJ: Wiley, 2010. Print. 133.

3. Ibid.

4. Alessio Fasano. "Genetics and Epidemiology of Celiac Disease." n.d. PDF file. 3 June 2011.

5. "Overview of Celiac Disease." *The University of Chicago Celiac Disease Center*. The University of Chicago Celiac Disease Center, 15 Aug. 2007. PDF file. 8 June 2011.

CHAPTER 3. FROM BAD TO WORSE: COMPLICATIONS

1. "Infertility and Celiac Disease." *National Foundation for Celiac Awareness*. National Foundation for Celiac Awareness, 17 Mar. 2011. Web. 13 Jan. 2011.

CHAPTER 4. I HAVE WHAT? TESTS AND DIAGNOSIS

None.

CHAPTER 5. LIFE WITHOUT GLUTEN: TREATMENT

1. A. R. Lee et al. "Economic Burden of a Gluten-Free Diet. *Journal of Human Nutrition and Dietetics* 20 (2007): 423–430. PDF file. 7 June 2011.

2. "What is Celiac Disease?" *National Foundation for Celiac Awareness*. National Foundation for Celiac Awareness, 11 Mar. 2011. PDF file. 23 Jan. 2011.

3. Brian Metzler. "Amy Begley: A Study in Tenacity." *Running Times*. Running Times Magazine, Dec. 2010. Web. 20 Jan. 2011.

SOURCE NOTES CONTINUED

CHAPTER 6. MAKING CHANGES AT HOME

1. Karyn James. Personal interview. 20 Jan. 2011.

2. "Living With Celiac Disease." *The University of Chicago Celiac Disease Center*. The University of Chicago Celiac Disease Center, n.d. Web. 23 Jan 2011.

3. Cameron Stevens. Personal interview. 20 Jan. 2011.

CHAPTER 7. NAVIGATING IN A GLUTEN-FILLED WORLD

1. Marina Keegan. "Celiac Patient Education Information: Ask the Teen!" *Children's Hospital Boston*. Children's Hospital Boston, 12 July 2010. Web. 23 Jan. 2010.

2. Christine P. Personal interview. 20 Jan. 2011.

CHAPTER 8. I CAN DO THIS: COPING AND THE FUTURE

1. Ruth Gonzalez. Personal interview. 17 Jan. 2011.

INDEX

ABOUT THE AUTHOR

Dale-Marie Bryan lives on a small farm with her husband, cats, and dogs. She enjoys writing food-related fiction and nonfiction for children and teenagers. This is her fourth book.

PHOTO CREDITS

iStockphoto, cover, 3, 20; Piotr Marcinski/Shutterstock Images, 8; Monkey Business Images/Shutterstock Images, 11, 43, 54; Shutterstock Images, 14, 83, 90, 93, 94; Marie C. Fields/Shutterstock Images, 17; DEA Picture Library/Getty Images, 23; Linda Bucklin/Bigstock, 25; Sebastian Kaulitzki/ Shutterstock Images, 27; Elena Elisseeva/Shutterstock Images, 30, 96; Catherine Yeulet/iStockphoto, 32; Otna Ydur/ Shutterstock Images, 37; Tom Hahn/iStockphoto, 40; Paul Kline/iStockphoto, 45; Fotolia, 47; Joseph Abbott/iStockphoto, 49; Nicole S. Young/iStockphoto, 51; Rohit Seth/Shutterstock Images, 59; Fotolia, 61; Kim Gunkel/iStockphoto, 65; Pete Saloutos/Shutterstock Images, 68; Joe Belanger/iStockphoto, 72; Ju-Lee/iStockphoto, 74; Sean Locke/iStockphoto, 76; Ivonne Wierink/Fotolia, 79; Aldo Murillo/iStockphoto, 86